Communities Work Together

Working as a Team

Tana Hensley

COMPUTER SCIENCE For the REAL World™

Rosen Classroom™

Published in 2018 by The Rosen Publishing Group, Inc.
29 East 21st Street, New York, NY 10010

Book Design: Jennifer Ryder-Talbot
Editor: Caitie McAneney

Photo Credits: Cover, 10 Rawpixel.com/Shutterstock.com; p. 4 Sean Xu/Shutterstock.com; p. 6 Frontpage/Shutterstock.com; p. 8 Lance Bellers/Shutterstock.com; p. 12 littleny/Shutterstock.com; p. 14 wavebreakmedia/Shutterstock.com.

ISBN: 9781538352366
6-pack ISBN: 9781508136880

Manufactured in the United States of America

CPSIA Compliance Information: Batch #WS18RC: For Further Information contact Rosen Publishing, New York, New York at 1-800-237-9932

Table of Contents

ERECTED·BY·THE·PEOPLE·CITY

What's Local Government?

Have you ever **participated** in your local government? The federal government is responsible for the whole nation. Each state government takes responsibility for its state. Local government is in charge of a smaller community, such as a town or city. Local governments are often responsible for taking care of parks, police, buses, and streets.

VOTE
HERE

Voting Is Important

It takes a lot of work to keep a city or town running smoothly. Local governments have several leaders, or officials. These may include mayors and council members. Community members **elect** these officials. When you are 18 years old, you can vote for your local government officials. Voting is one way of working together to build a strong community.

TOWN HALL

Local Leaders

What do local government officials do? They work with other officials and community members to make a difference. Mayors oversee **departments** and help make decisions about the community. Council members make local laws and decisions. They usually work at a city hall or a town hall. First, these officials must learn about their community's wants and needs. It's time to work together!

Make Your Voice Heard!

Some community members participate in public meetings. Public meetings often take place at town hall or city hall. Community members are able to meet with their local government officials. They can talk to leaders about things that are important to them. Other people write letters or make phone calls to their officials. Some people start **petitions** about an issue.

Get to Work!

Sometimes people support a certain cause. They may form or join a group that works to solve a problem. A group that's interested in bringing a community together may make a community garden. A group that's interested in after-school programs may start a sports club for kids. Each person in the group will have a certain job to help the cause.

Make a Difference

Local government is all about community members and government officials working together. Officials have the power to pass laws and make decisions. Community members have the power to fight for causes that are important to them. They might even form groups that work together for the same causes. You can make a difference in your community!

Glossary

department: A division of a government.

elect: To choose for a position in a government by voting.

participate: To take part in something.

petition: A written request signed by many people asking the government to take an action.

Index